Table of
CONTENTS

CHAPTER 1

The Eating Machines 5

CHAPTER 2

The Tropical Rain Forest Biome... 13

CHAPTER 3

Tropical Rain Forest
Communities 20

CHAPTER 4

Tropical Rain Forest Plants........... 26

CHAPTER 5

Tropical Rain Forest Animals 36

Words to Know......................... 45

Learn More............................. 47
(Books and Internet Addresses)

Index.................................. 48

The lush,
tropical
rain forest
has many
layers
of leaves.

THE TROPICAL RAIN FOREST

A Web of Life

Philip Johansson

 Enslow Publishers, Inc.

40 Industrial Road	PO Box 38
Box 398	Aldershot
Berkeley Heights, NJ 07922	Hants GU12 6BP
USA	UK

http://www.enslow.com

Library of Congress Cataloging-in-Publication Data

Johansson, Philip.
    The tropical rain forest : a web of life / Philip Johansson.
        v. cm. — (A world of biomes)
    Includes index.
    Contents: The eating machines — The making of a biome — Biome communities — Tropical rain
        forest plants — Tropical rain forest animals.
    ISBN 0-7660-2199-8 (hardcover)
    1. Rain forest ecology—Juvenile literature. [1. Rain forests. 2. Rain forest ecology. 3. Ecology.]
        I. Title. II. Series.
    QH541.5.R27J62 2004
    577.34—dc21

                                            2003006481

To Our Readers: We have done our best to make sure all Internet Addresses in this book were active and appropriate when we went to press. However, the author and the publisher have no control over and assume no liability for the material available on those Internet sites or on other Web sites they may link to. Any comments or suggestions can be sent by e-mail to comments@enslow.com or to the address on the back cover.

Photo Credits: © 1999, Artville, LLC, pp. 10–11; © Theo Allofs/Visuals Unlimited, pp. 31, 42; © Norris Blake/ Visuals Unlimited, p. 34, 35; Nic Bishop, p. 9; © Corel Corporation, p. 25 (unless otherwise credited in book); Dr. Lee Dyer, pp. 6, 43; © Jacques Jangoux/Visuals Unlimited, pp. 4, 16, 18, 24, 28; © 1999 Frans Lanting, pp. 14, 33, 38, 40; © Ken Lucas/Visuals Unlimited, p. 39, 44; © Joe McDonald/Visuals Unlimited, p. 23; © Greg Neise/Visuals Unlimited, p. 17; © Fritz Polking/Visuals Unlimited, p. 32; © David Sieren/Visuals Unlimited, p. 29; © Inga Spence/Visuals Unlimited, p. 22.

Illustration credits: *Heck's Pictorial Archive of Art and Architecture*, except for Dover Publications, Inc., pp. 5, 13, 20, 26, 36.

Cover Photos: © Theo Allofs/Visuals Unlimited (top left, bottom right); © 1993 Frans Lanting (top right); © 1999 Frans Lanting (bottom left).

Dr. Lee Dyer is an ecologist and evolutionary biologist from Tulane University in New Orleans. He studies the ecology of caterpillars in the rain forests of Costa Rica and Ecuador. The volunteers depicted in Chapter 1 are from Earthwatch Institute, a nonprofit organization. Earthwatch supports field science and conservation through the participation of the public. See www.earthwatch.org for more information.

The EATING MACHINES

Caterpillars are leaf-eating machines. A small group of caterpillars can strip a tree almost bare in just a few days. Lush, tropical rain forests, with layers upon layers of leaves, are a caterpillar's dream.

Dr. Lee Dyer is a scientist who studies rain forest caterpillars. He does not have to look hard to find them.

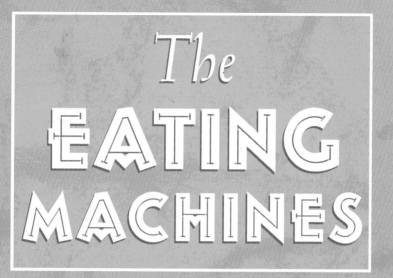

Dr. Lee Dyer and his team found this fuzzy caterpillar in a rain forest in Ecuador.

Dr. Dyer is walking through a rain forest in Ecuador, South America, with a team of six volunteers. They are looking for trees with leaves that have been eaten. Layers of green plants grow on either side of the path as high as they can see. The leaves blot out most of the tropical sunlight. Water drips from the trees after the recent rain. The air is thick with moisture. Bright sounds of calling birds and monkeys fill the forest.

"Whoa, here we go," says Dr. Dyer. He has just turned over a leaf. Underneath he finds a red-legged, red-headed caterpillar covered with soft white fur. "I've never seen this one before," says Dr. Dyer. Everyone agrees that it is most unusual.

One of the volunteers carefully puts the caterpillar in a bag. The fuzzy creature will be studied

back at the field laboratory. Another volunteer collects a sample of the leaf it was eating. They will identify the plant later. Meanwhile, the volunteers excitedly return to their caterpillar hunting.

Tropical Plenty

Thousands of different kinds of caterpillars live in tropical rain forests. There are at least twenty thousand varieties just in the tiny South American nation of Ecuador. That is twice the number found in the entire United States, which is much larger.

Scientists have not even discovered and named most tropical rain forest caterpillars. Of the 121 distinct caterpillars that Dr. Dyer's team collects in three weeks, none of them is familiar. Caterpillars become moths and butterflies, and most of these have been named. Dyer wants to discover which moth or butterfly each caterpillar becomes.

Back at the field laboratory, the volunteers unpack the few dozen caterpillars they have collected

today. They write down information on each insect, such as where it was found, how it behaved, and what kind of plant it was eating. Then they put the caterpillars into separate bags to develop into butterflies and moths. For now, the first caterpillar found by Dr. Dyer that day is named a "red-legged fuzzy wuzzy."

Full of Surprises

Dr. Dyer has been studying rain forest caterpillars for more than ten years. He is still amazed at how many surprises the rain forest holds. Each kind of caterpillar has a different role in the rain forest. Each eats a certain kind of plant, and may be eaten by a particular predator. Dr. Dyer wants to discover the role of each kind of caterpillar in the rain forest.

Caterpillars are just one of the many animals that make up tropical rain forests. Scientists like Dr. Dyer are trying to learn about the relationships between forest plants and animals to understand how the rain forest works.

Dr. Lee Dyer climbs into the rain forest treetops to collect caterpillars.

What Is a Biome?

The tropical rain forest is one kind of biome. A biome is a large region of the Earth where certain

LEGEND

- Tundra
- Taiga
- Temperate forest
- Grassland
- Desert
- Rain forest
- Chaparral
- Mountain zone
- Polar ice

Ecuador

Biomes

plants and animals live. They survive there because they are well suited to the temperatures and amounts of rainfall found in that area.

of the World

Each biome has plants that may not be found in other biomes. For example, trees grow in forests, but not in deserts. Cacti grow in deserts, but not in the tundra. The animals that eat these plants help form the community of a biome. Exploring biomes is a good way to understand how these communities work. In this book you will learn about the plants and animals that live in the tropical rain forest biome.

The Tropical RAIN FOREST BIOME

Tropical rain forests

form a belt of lush, green growth around the middle of the world. They grow near the equator, in parts of Central and South America, Central and West Africa, Southeast Asia, and Australia. The largest is the Amazon Rain Forest in South America. It covers an area larger than one third of the United States.

The sunlight and moisture are usually constant and plentiful, so the growing conditions are ideal for many types of plants. Inside the rain forest, there is an amazing assortment of trees and other plants. They fill the forest with layers of big shiny leaves, from the ground to the treetops more than one hundred feet above. With all these layers, most of the forest floor is in the shade all day.

A Special Place

Tropical rain forests make up one fifth of the world's forests. They cover only a tiny fraction of Earth's land (about 6 percent), but they contain more than half of the planet's living plants and animals. For example, while all of North America is home to 650 species of birds, the tiny tropical nation of Panama has 1,100. More than three quarters of all insect species live in tropical rain forests.

Many plants and animals in the tropical rain forest are very specialized in their habits. This means that they only eat certain foods, or live on certain trees, or even just on certain parts of certain trees. For example, one kind of ant in South America is only found inside *Cecropia* trees, and lives on food provided by the trees. Some orchids in Madagascar hide their nectar at the end of a long spur, where only the long-tongued hawk moth can reach it. These specializations make the tropical rain forest's web of life a complex one.

There are many orchids in the rain forest. Some orchids are pollinated by only one type of insect.

Rain Forest Weather

Another reason for the diversity of life in tropical rain forests is the tropical climate. Tropical rain forests do not have the same seasons found in colder regions. Since they are near the equator, tropical rain forests tend to be warm throughout the year. Most rain forest temperatures average from 70 to 85 degrees Fahrenheit (about 20 to 30 degrees Celsius) any time of year.

As you might guess, rain is important in rain forests. Rain forests get from 80 to 400 inches (200 to 1,000 centimeters) of rain every year, much more than any other biome. Sometimes it may rain 2 inches (5 centimeters) in an hour—as much as a desert might

The air is very humid in the rain forest.

*Rain begins
to fall in the
rain forest.*

get in a whole year. Although the temperature is constant, most rain forests have a short period that is less wet than the rest of the year.

Water Gets Recycled

Rain forests recycle water. During the morning, the sun heats up the forest. Water vapor, or steam, rises from the dripping leaves and humid air under the trees. The rising water vapor forms clouds over the forest. When enough moisture collects in the clouds, sometime in the afternoon, it drops as rain. There are rain forests where this daily downpour is so predictable you could set your watch by it.

✓ **Abundant life:** Tropical rain forests hold half of the Earth's plants and animals on only 6 percent of the land.

✓ **Specialized roles:** With so many kinds of animals, many have very particular roles. The food web is complex, with many more specialized relationships than in other biomes.

✓ **Dark forest floor:** Sunlight is scarce beneath the layers of the rain forest.

TROPICAL RAIN FOREST FACTS

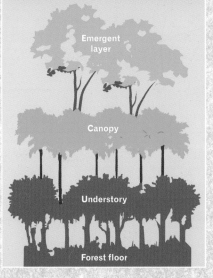

Emergent layer

Canopy

Understory

Forest floor

✓ **Tropical temperatures:** Temperatures are always warm, averaging 70 to 85 degrees Fahrenheit (about 20 to 30 degrees Celsius).

✓ **Plenty of rain:** Between 80 and 400 inches (200 to 1,000 centimeters) of rain each year, more than any other biome.

✓ **Recycled water:** Moisture from the forest rises in the morning and is dropped as rain later in the day.

Tropical RAIN FOREST COMMUNITIES

Communities are the groups of living things found together in a place. Within a community, some plants and animals depend on others. Each living thing has a particular role in the community.

Energy Flow in a Rain Forest

Plants in the rain forest trap energy from sunlight for their food. Then they use the energy to make sugar. The sugar is made

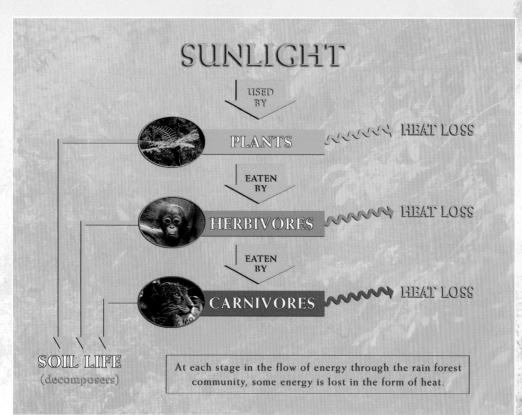

SUNLIGHT

USED BY

PLANTS ∿∿∿∿ HEAT LOSS

EATEN BY

HERBIVORES ∿∿∿∿ HEAT LOSS

EATEN BY

CARNIVORES ∿∿∿∿ HEAT LOSS

SOIL LIFE
(decomposers)

At each stage in the flow of energy through the rain forest community, some energy is lost in the form of heat.

from carbon dioxide (a gas in the air) and water from the air or soil. Plants later use the energy in the sugars to build new leaves, stems, roots, and flowers.

Some animals, such as caterpillars and sloths, eat these plants. Animals that eat only plants are called herbivores. Herbivores get their energy from plants. Other animals, called carnivores, eat herbivores. Jaguars, tree frogs, and spiders are carnivores. Carnivores get their energy from eating the meat of

other animals. Omnivores, such as birds called pitas, eat both plants and animals.

When plants and animals die, soil animals and fungi get to work. They help break down the dead plants and animals. This releases nutrients back into the soil. Earthworms, beetles, fungi, microbes, and other soil life do this job. They are called decomposers.

The Food Web

The flow of energy from the sun to plants to herbivores to carnivores to decomposers follows a pattern called a food web. Like a spider's web, it connects the plants and animals of a community in a complicated network of who eats whom. For example, banana plants make food from the sun's energy. Pig-like animals called peccaries eat the banana plants. Jaguars might eat the peccaries. When the jaguar dies, the decomposers break down the dead animal and release nutrients back to the food web.

▲ A three-toed sloth climbs a tree in the Amazon. The sloth is a herbivore.

The jaguar is a predator in the rain forest. ➤

Tree ferns are an important part of the rain forest food web. The plants gather energy from the sun.

Together, plants and animals pass energy through the biome community. They also use some of the energy to live. At each stage of the food web, some energy is lost as the animals use it. Plants need to trap more energy from the sun to keep the community alive.

Learning from Biomes

Exploring biomes like the tropical rain forest is a good way to learn how communities work. By looking at the plants and animals in any biome, you will see how they all need each other. If you take any plant or animal away, it could change how the community works. To protect the Earth's future, it is important to learn about biomes and the plants and animals that bring them to life.

SOME PLANTS AND ANIMALS IN THE
RAIN FOREST FOOD WEB

PLANTS	HERBIVORES	CARNIVORES

Eaten by →   **Eaten by** →

PLANTS	HERBIVORES	CARNIVORES
Mahogany Trees	Insects	Anacondas
Avocados	Capybaras	
Figs	Tapirs	Caiman
Palms	Monkeys	
Tree Ferns	Macaws	Jaguars
Philodendron	Toucans	
Epiphytes	Sloths	Cougars
Lianas	Katydids	Tree Frogs
Orchids	Caterpillars	
Ferns		Lizards

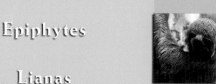

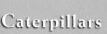

SOIL LIFE

Worms   Bacteria   Fungi

Chapter 4

Tropical
RAIN FOREST
PLANTS

If you piled all the world's plants in one place, one third of the pile would come from the tropical rain forests. And if you made a list of every known plant variety in the world, more than half would live in tropical rain forests. While entire forests in colder regions usually have five to ten kinds of trees, one patch

of rain forest smaller than a football field can have as many as one hundred different varieties of trees. Hundreds of other kinds of plants grow among them.

The leaves of most rain forest trees stay green and soak up the sun's energy all year. Each tree or other plant makes flowers and fruit at its own time of year instead of all of them doing it at the same time. This makes the forest a place where plenty of food can be found most of the year for the animals living there.

Layers of the Forest

Tropical rain forests grow in several layers, like layers in a cake. One of the reasons that there can be so many different living things in the rain forest is that there are so many layers. Each layer is a special place for both plants and animals to live.

The highest trees are called emergents. These stick out from the top of the treetops, or canopy. The canopy is where most treetops come together. Emergent trees act like a giant umbrella over the rest of the forest.

The obeche tree of West Africa, an emergent tree, can tower to a height of 200 feet (60 meters) and grow to 22 feet (7 meters) wide at the base.

Emergent trees are the tallest trees in the rain forest. They stick out from the treetops.

The next layer down is the canopy, between 60 and 100 feet (18 and 30 meters). Mahogany, Brazil nut, silk-cotton, and avocado are all trees that grow in the canopy. As much as 90 percent of all the living things in the rain forest, both plants and animals, are found here.

The layer below the canopy is the understory. It has many kinds of shrubs and small trees. Dwarf palms grow here, alongside spreading tree ferns, breadfruits, coffee trees, and cacao trees, the source of cocoa and chocolate. As little as 2 percent of the bright tropical sunlight gets down this far, so plants grow slowly.

Some saplings of larger trees wait here for a chance to grow up into the canopy. When a large tree falls and opens a gap in the canopy, letting sunlight through, small trees have a burst of growth to fill it.

The forest floor makes up the final layer of a tropical rain forest. Very little grows on the forest floor because so little sunlight reaches this area. But ferns and other plants, as well as fungi, can live in the dappled light at the base of the forest. *Thismia* is a flowering plant that is not green and cannot make its own food like most plants. Instead it feeds on decaying matter on the forest floor. *Rafflesia*, the largest flower on Earth with a bloom reaching three feet across, grows

Understory plants grow beneath the rain forest canopy. This breadfruit tree is part of the understory.

◆ **29** ◆

on the forest floor of Southeast Asian rain forests. There it lives off the roots of jungle vines.

Reaching for the Sky

Rain forest trees and other plants have many special features to help them reach the canopy, where sunlight is the strongest. One example is "air plants," or epiphytes. They sit high on the trunks and limbs of tall trees. These plants use the trees for support. They are called air plants because they are not rooted in soil; they get moisture and nutrients from the air and dust. Many orchids and philodendrons are epiphytes.

Lianas, or vines, grow from the ground up to the canopy by climbing trees. Only after they reach the bright light of the canopy do these lianas make flowers and fruit. The strangler fig starts out as an epiphyte, growing on a tree limb. But then it sends several roots down the trunk of the tree. After putting its roots into the ground, the strangler continues to

The rain forest canopy contains many different trees, such as Brazil nut, avocado, and mahogany.

grow until the tree is smothered and dies. The strangler is left in its place, where it enjoys the light of the upper canopy.

Flowers and Fruits

The wind rarely reaches below the rain forest canopy. Few rain forest trees rely on the wind to move their pollen from flower to flower. That is why most plants have large, bright flowers. The colorful flowers with their sweet aromas attract the many insects, birds, and mammals that live in the rain forest. These animals in turn pollinate the plants.

Because there is little wind below the canopy, rain forest trees also need another way to spread their

Epiphytes sit on the trunks and limbs of tall trees. This is an air plant called a bromeliad.

seeds around the forest. They often have large fruits, which also attract many animals. Seeds are carried all around the forest by birds, mammals, reptiles, and even fish. They all eat the juicy fruits. Agoutis, large rodents in Central and South American rain forests, play a key role in spreading tree seeds. They bury them in the ground for storage, and often forget where they hid them.

Large, bright flowers attract insects, birds, and mammals.

Coffee plants grow in the rain forest. The coffee fruit is called a berry.

Humans Use the Plants, Too

Humans also use many of the rain forest flowers and fruits that attract animals in the forest. For instance, bananas, avocados, pineapples, oranges, coffee, cocoa, vanilla, and many oils used in perfumes come from rain forest plants. Almost three quarters of the plants identified as useful in treating cancer come from tropical rain forests.

PLANT FACTS

✓ **Green all year**: Because the climate is generally warm and wet, trees and plants stay green throughout the year.

✓ **Diverse trees**: Rain forests have many more kinds of trees than any other kind of forest.

✓ **Forest layers**: Trees and plants form layers, including emergents, canopy, understory, and forest floor.

✓ **Showy flowers**: Many plants have large, bright flowers to attract insects, birds, and mammals to pollinate them.

✓ **Life in the canopy**: Many plants and animals live in the canopy. Some plants, such as epiphytes, lianas, and stranglers, have special adaptations for reaching the canopy.

✓ **Life in the shade**: Plants living beneath the canopy are adapted to low light. They have big leaves for collecting sunlight.

✓ **Fleshy fruits**: Many plants have large, tasty fruits to attract birds, mammals, and even fish, which spread their seeds to other parts of the forest.

Tropical RAIN FOREST ANIMALS

Just as there are many more kinds of trees and plants in the rain forest than in any other biome, the same is true for animals. An amazing variety of animals dwells in the rain forest. They live off the energy and nutrients stored in the diverse forest plants.

Four square miles (about 10 square kilometers) of tropical rain forest contains as many as 125 kinds of mammals,

◆ 36 ◆

400 kinds of birds, 100 kinds of reptiles, 60 kinds of amphibians, and 150 kinds of butterflies. That is more than you will find in many countries in colder climates. One scientist found fifty species of ants in one square yard (one square meter) of rain forest floor.

Life in the Trees

Many animals have adaptations for living high in the trees, where they find most of their food. Monkeys, for instance, are able to climb trees with ease. They have long arms and strong hands to swing from branch to branch, and excellent balance for leaping among the treetops. Monkeys in Central and South America also have tails that can wrap around branches and support their weight.

Animals that you might not expect to live in the trees can be found in the rain forest canopy. A small mammal called the common tree shrew lives in Southeast Asian rain forests. Although it eats insects as its shrew relatives living on the ground do, it climbs

trees like a squirrel. The flying dragon of Indonesia is a lizard with large flaps of skin on either side of its belly, which it uses to glide from tree to tree.

There are even frogs that live in rain forest trees. Some tadpoles live in the water that collects in epiphyte leaves. Tadpoles stay in this water and grow into frogs.

Poison dart frogs are tree frogs that have a powerful poison on their skin. Their bright colors

▲ *With its bright colors, this poison dart frog warns predators.*

◄ *Woolly spider monkeys live in rain forest trees of Brazil.*

warn predators not to eat them. Poison dart frogs got their name because some hunters use the poison on their blow darts.

Another unusual creature that lives in the treetops is the sloth. This slow-moving mammal hangs from the branches by long, hooked claws. There it slowly eats leaves, and may spend several days in one tree. Some even have green algae, or tiny plants, living in their fur. This helps them blend in with the foliage.

The Forest Web

There are many large, fleshy fruits in the rain forest. Lots of animals rely on this food. Large birds with bright tropical colors, such as toucans, quetzals, and macaws, feast on fruits in the canopy. Fruit bats, like the flying fox, enjoy the fruits in the trees as well. Rodents and peccaries (large mammals related to pigs) eat the fruits that fall to the ground. Many insects also feast on fallen fruits that rot on the ground.

Monkeys make a banquet of the green leaves that fill the rain forest. Countless insects, such as caterpillars, beetles, and katydids, also chew on leaves in the canopy. Katydids are large grasshopper-like insects that live in the trees. There are hundreds of varieties, many of which have wings that look like rain forest leaves.

On the ground, large mammals munch on the leaves in the understory. These mammals include tapirs, which are six-foot-long mammals found in South American rain forests. Tapirs use a long upper lip to

Colorful macaws flock together in Peru.

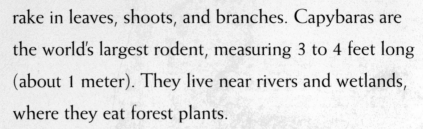

A katydid's wings look like rain forest leaves.

rake in leaves, shoots, and branches. Capybaras are the world's largest rodent, measuring 3 to 4 feet long (about 1 meter). They live near rivers and wetlands, where they eat forest plants.

Carnivores, in turn, prey on these plant eaters. Tree frogs, lizards, birds, and other insect-eaters find plentiful food among the hordes of rain forest insects. In fact, many insects, such as ants and wasps, feed on other insects as well. Huge snakes called anacondas hunt small mammals by wrapping around them and squeezing until the mammals cannot breathe. Caiman, large relatives of crocodiles, hunt for animals that come to the water to drink. Jaguars, the largest cat in the Americas, stalk peccaries, tapirs, and other large prey in the rain forest understory.

Caterpillars in the Web

Like every other plant or animal in the rain forest, caterpillars have a special role in the forest food web. For instance, some of the caterpillars found by Dr. Dyer and his volunteer assistants eat only one kind of plant. Others eat a wide variety of plants. Although they are small, caterpillars can have a big impact on how the forest community works.

The adult stage of the "red-legged fuzzy wuzzy" collected by Dr. Dycr and his assistants was eventually identified as a small, brown moth in the

genus *Apatelodes*. This fuzzy caterpillar eats several kinds of plants, but it is often found on *Piper* plants that are commonly found in the rain forest. The caterpillar is an important plant eater and, in turn, is a good food for many birds and other insect eaters.

The "red-legged fuzzy wuzzy" collected by Dr. Lee Dyer turned into this small, brown moth, an Apatelodes.

Dr. Dyer's work with the hundreds of caterpillars he has found will help scientists understand some of the special relationships that make the rain forest work.

ANIMAL FACTS

✓ Lots of animals: Tropical rain forests have the highest diversity of animals of any biome. A four-square-mile area of tropical rain forest contains as many as 125 kinds of mammals and 150 kinds of butterflies.

✓ Tree life: Many mammals have adaptations for living high in the trees, such as sharp claws, long arms, good balance, and loud calls.

✓ Unusual animals: Many unusual animals live in the rain forest. These include lizards that glide, frogs that live entirely in trees and are covered with poison, and sloths with algae living in their fur.

✓ Fruit eaters: Many animals, including birds, bats, large mammals, and insects, rely on the abundant fruits and flowers of the rain forest.

WORDS TO KNOW

adaptation—A trait of a plant or animal that helps it to live under certain conditions.

biome—An area of the earth defined by the kinds of plants that live there.

canopy—The upper layer of the forest where the tops of the trees come together.

carnivore—An animal that eats other animals.

caterpillar—Immature or larval stage of a moth or butterfly.

climate—The patterns of temperature and precipitation that occur through the year.

community—All the plants and animals living and interacting in any area.

decay—The breakdown of dead plants or animals into nutrients by bacteria, fungi, and other living things.

decomposers—Soil animals and fungi that help break down dead plants and animals and release nutrients back into the soil.

emergent—A tree that grows above the protection of the canopy, over one hundred feet above ground.

epiphyte—A plant that grows on the limbs of trees. It uses the tree for support and gets moisture and nutrients from the air.

food web—The transfer of energy from the sun to plants to herbivores to carnivores, and back to decomposers.

habitat—The area where a certain plant or animal normally lives, eats, and finds shelter.

herbivore—An animal that eats plants.

liana—A woody vine that grows from the ground up to the sunlight in the canopy.

nutrients—Chemicals necessary for plants and animals to live.

omnivore—An animal that eats plants and animals.

parasite—An animal that lives on or in another animal, and gets its nutrients directly from the animal it lives on.

precipitation—Water falling in a given area in the form of rain, snow, fog, or hail.

predator—An animal that hunts other animals for food.

strangler—A plant that sends roots from the top of a host tree down to the ground, strangling the tree in the process.

tropical—Relating to a region close to the equator, with a climate that is always warm.

understory—Small trees and shrubs growing under the canopy of the forest.

LEARN MORE

FURTHER READING

Berger, Melvin and Gilda. *Does It Always Rain in the Rain Forest?* New York: Scholastic, Inc., 2001.

Cheshire, Gerard. *The Tropical Forest.* New York: Crabtree Publishing Company, 2001.

Collard, Sneed B., III, *The Forest in the Clouds.* Watertown, Mass.: Charlesbridge Publishing, 2000.

Lyman, Francesca, ed. *Inside the Dzanga Sangha Rainforest.* New York: Workman Publishing Company, 1998.

Taylor, Barbara. *In the Rainforest.* New York: Barron's Educational Series, 1999.

Wilkes, Angela. *Rain Forest.* New York: Kingfisher, 2002.

INTERNET ADDRESSES

Missouri Botanical Garden. *Biomes of the World.* "Rainforest." <http://mbgnet.mobot.org/sets/rforest/index.htm>

Woodward, Susan L. *Major Biomes of the World.* "Tropical Broadleaf Evergreen Forest: The Rainforest." <http://www.runet.edu/~swoodwar/CLASSES/GEOG235/biomes/rainforest/rainfrst.html>

INDEX

A

agoutis, 33
air plants, 30
Amazon Rain Forest, 13
amphibians, 37
anacondas, 42
ants, 15, 37, 42
avocados, 28, 34

B

bananas, 22, 34
bats, 41
beetles, 41
biome, 10–12
birds, 15, 32, 33, 37, 41, 42, 43
butterflies, 7–8, 37

C

caiman, 42
canopy, 27–29, 30, 32
capybaras, 42
carnivores, 21–22, 42
caterpillars, 5–8, 21, 41, 43–44
climate, 17
cocoa, 28, 34
coffee, 28, 34
common tree shrew, 37
communities, 12, 20, 24, 43

D

decomposers, 22
Dyer, Lee, 5–8, 43, 44

E

emergents, 27–28
epiphytes, 30
equator, 17

F

ferns, 29
fish, 33
flowers, 27, 32
flying dragon, 39
food web, 22, 24
forest floor, 29
frogs, 21, 39–40, 42
fruits, 27, 33, 41
fungi, 22, 29

H

herbivores, 21, 22

I

insects, 15, 32, 37, 41, 42

J

jaguars, 21, 22, 42

K

katydids, 41

L

layers, 14, 27–28
lianas, 30
lizards, 42

M

macaws, 41
mahogany, 28
mammals, 32, 33, 36, 41–42
monkeys, 37, 41
moths, 7–8, 15, 43

N

nutrients, 22

O

omnivores, 22
oranges, 34

orchids, 15, 30

P

peccaries, 22, 41, 42
philodendrons, 30
pineapples, 34
poison dart frogs, 39–40
pollen, 32
pitas, 22

Q

quetzals, 41

R

rainfall, 11, 17–18
reptiles, 33, 37
rodents, 33, 41, 42

S

sloths, 21, 40
soil animals, 22
spiders, 21
strangler figs, 30
sunlight, 14, 20, 28

T

tapirs, 41–42
temperatures, 11, 17–18
toucans, 41
trees, 14, 26–29
tree ferns, 28

U

understory, 28

V

vanilla, 34

W

wasps, 42